THIS BOOK BELONGS TO

COLOR TEST PAGES

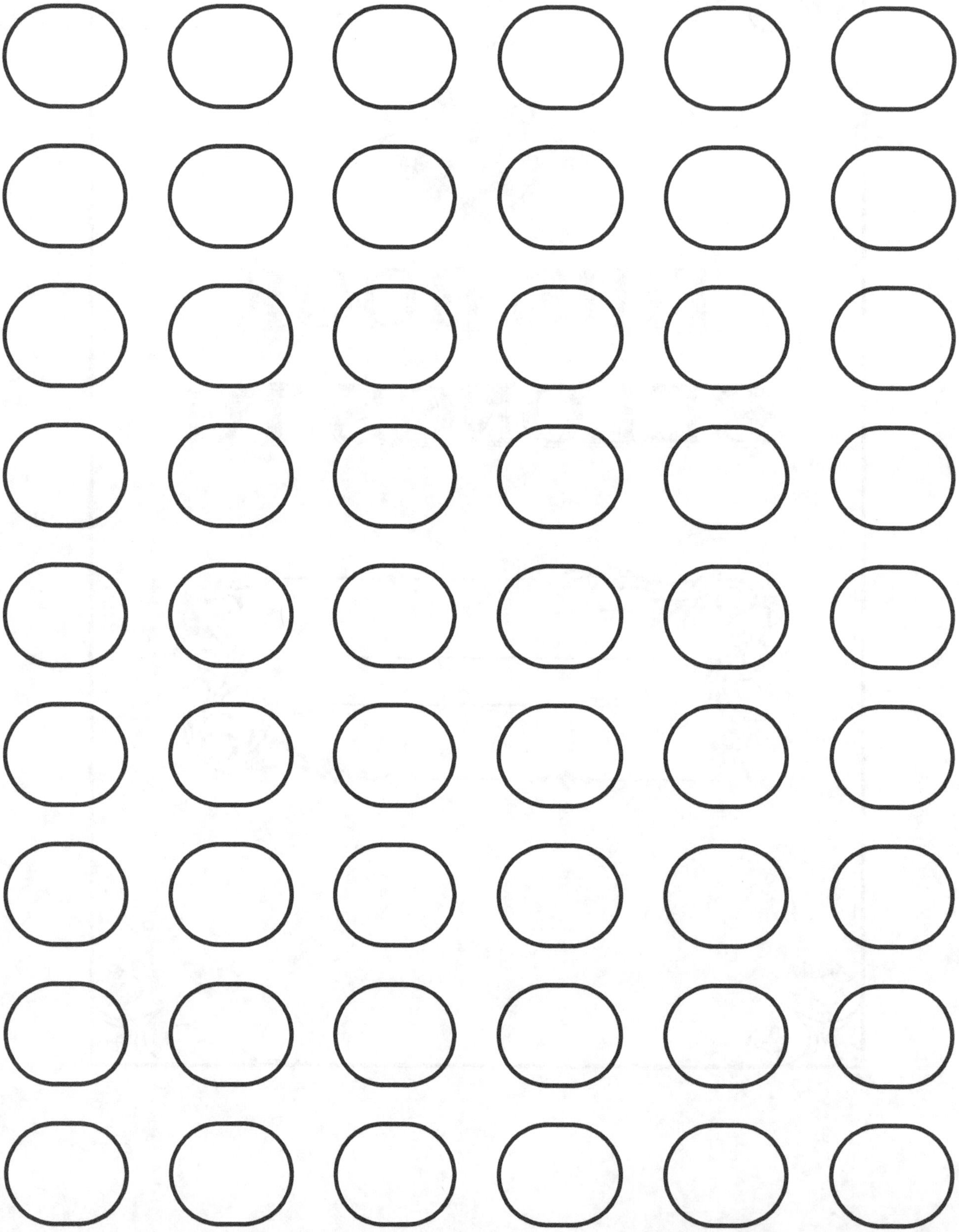

RIP

HALLOWEEN

HAPPY HALLO
WEEN

TRICK
OR
TREAT!

HALLOWEEN
PARTY

TRICK
OR
TREAT

Happy Halloween

RIP
RIP
RIP
Poison

RIP
RIP
RIP
RIP
RIP
RIP
RIP
RIP
Poison

RIP

RIP

RIP
RIP

HALLOWEEN
R.I.P

HALLOWEEN

www.ingramcontent.com/pod-product-compliance
Lightning Source LLC
Chambersburg PA
CBHW081416080526
44589CB00016B/2560